Bring home the bacon - fry it up in a pan!

Or not. Cook your bacon any way you like, but here's the skinny on the best techniques to get it golden brown and crisp.

Bakin' Bacon

Arrange bacon strips on a foil-lined pan and bake in a 400° oven for 18 to 25 minutes (no preheating necessary).

Micro Magic Cover a plate with paper towels and line up bacon strips; cover with more paper towels and microwave on high for 45 to 60 seconds per strip.

Fry It Up In A Pan

Place bacon strips (or smaller pieces) in a cold skillet and fry on both sides over medium heat. Need crumbled bacon? Dice it before frying.

Porky Pointers

- One pound of sliced bacon contains 12 to 16 thick cut strips (⅛″) and 16 to 20 thinner strips. Choose thin strips when wrapping bacon around other foods.

- Always drain cooked bacon on paper towels to absorb excess grease.

- For easy clean-up, line baking pans with foil or parchment paper. After cooking, let the bacon grease set up and then just throw the liner and grease away.

- Wash pans in hot soapy water to cut the grease.

Oink-a-Moly Guacamole

Ingredients

8 bacon strips

2 ripe avocados

⅔ C. chopped tomato

⅓ C. chopped fresh cilantro

¼ C. chopped onion

½ minced jalapeño pepper

Fresh lime juice

Salt and black pepper

Cook the bacon until crisp; drain and let cool. Crumble the bacon and discard the grease.

Pit and peel the avocados; mash them up with a fork. Stir in the tomato, cilantro, onion, jalapeño, and bacon. Add a few splashes of lime juice and stir well. Season with salt and pepper. Serve promptly with chips. *Makes 1 to 1½ cups dip.* ◐

fun fact
One 200-pound porker can provide about 20 pounds of bacon.

BACON

ODE TO BACON

BACON, you're amazing.
I love your salty ways.

Your wavy curves and crispy crunch
have started quite a craze.

Your aroma is alluring.
Your taste is matched by none.

Crumbled or au naturel,
cooking with you is fun.

Melted cheese? Yes indeed.
You make a lovely pair.

On chocolate? In bread? With chips?
None can quite compare.

You taste great with everything—
you're versatile and grand.

In fact, you just might be the greatest
food in all the land.

Printed in the United States of America
by G&R Publishing Co.

Distributed By:

Products

507 Industrial Street
Waverly, IA 50677

ISBN-13: 978-1-56383-497-4
Item #7109

Cool Blue Bacon Dip

Ingredients

4 bacon strips

½ C. sour cream

4 oz. crumbled blue cheese

3 oz. cream cheese, softened

2 T. minced fresh onion

¼ tsp. hot sauce, or more to taste

Salt and black pepper

Chopped fresh parsley, optional

Cook the bacon until crisp; drain and let cool. Crumble the bacon and discard the grease.

In a blender container or food processor bowl, combine sour cream, blue cheese, cream cheese, onion, and hot sauce; process until smooth, stopping to scrape down the sides occasionally. Transfer to a bowl and stir in most of the bacon; season with salt and pepper. Cover and chill for 2 hours. Let stand at room temperature for 15 minutes before serving. Sprinkle with the remaining bacon and parsley, if desired. Serve with fresh vegetables. *Makes 1½ cups dip.*

try this: *Score the skin of three cucumbers and slice into rounds, about 1˝ thick. Scoop out some of the seeds in each chunk with a melon baller and fill with chilled dip.*

Cheesy Bacon Bombs

Ingredients

- ¾ lb. block mozzarella or Pepper Jack cheese
- 1 (16.3 oz.) tube refrigerated Grands flaky layers biscuits
- Garlic salt, seasoned salt, or cayenne pepper to taste
- **16 bacon strips, cut in half**
- Canola oil for frying

Cheese makes everything better, even bacon!

Directions

Cut the cheese into 32 (¾″ to 1″) cubes. Quarter each biscuit, flatten, and sprinkle with seasoning as desired. Place one cheese cube on each biscuit piece and wrap dough around cheese, pinching to seal well. Wrap a bacon piece around each biscuit ball and secure with a toothpick.

Fill a large heavy pot with at least 2″ of oil and heat it to 350°. In small batches, fry the bacon-wrapped biscuit balls until bacon is crisp and biscuit is golden brown. Drain on paper towels. Serve warm. *Makes 32 appetizers.* ۞

try this: *Use cubes of Cheddar cheese and add some cooked, crumbled ground beef inside the biscuits for cheeseburger bombs.*

Cheeseburger Piggy Puffs

Ingredients

4 bacon strips

½ lb. lean ground beef

1½ C. biscuit baking mix

2 C. shredded Cheddar cheese

6 to 7 T. buttermilk

Heat oven to 400°. Cook the bacon until crisp; drain and let cool. Crumble the bacon and discard the grease.

In a skillet, cook ground beef over medium heat until crumbly; drain. In a bowl, combine the baking mix, cheese, and bacon. Stir in cooked beef. Add buttermilk and stir until just moistened. Shape into 1½″ balls. Place the balls 2″ apart on an ungreased rimmed baking sheet and bake 12 to 15 minutes, until golden brown and slightly puffed. *Makes 32 appetizers.* ◖

try this: *Make puffs ahead of time and freeze them. Reheat frozen puffs at 400° for 7 to 9 minutes.*

Hog-Wild Hummus

Ingredients

3 bacon strips

1 (15 oz.) can chickpeas
(garbanzo beans)

⅓ C. tahini (sesame paste)

2 T. lemon juice

1 tsp. minced garlic

2 T. chopped green onion

Salt and black pepper

Cook the bacon until crisp; drain and let cool. Reserve
1 tablespoon grease. Crumble the bacon and set all aside.

In a food processor bowl, combine chickpeas, tahini, reserved
bacon grease, lemon juice, and garlic; pulse until just smooth,
stopping to scrape down the sides as needed. Add ¼ cup water,
green onion, and bacon. Pulse until blended. Season with salt
and pepper. Chill well. Serve with fresh veggies and crisp bacon
strips. *Makes about 1½ cups.* ◖

fun fact
During WWII, leftover bacon grease was
sometimes used to make ammunition.

Bacon-Back Turtles

Ingredients

6 bacon strips

12 oz. pecan halves, toasted (about 96)

1 (13 oz.) pkg. caramels, unwrapped

Milk or half & half

1 (4 oz.) pkg. semi-sweet baking chocolate, chopped

Coarse salt, optional

Cover a cookie sheet with foil and coat with cooking spray. Cook bacon strips until crisp; drain and let cool. Break each strip into four equal pieces and set them aside.

On prepared cookie sheet, make clusters of four pecans with each pecan pointing in a different direction, like turtle legs. Heat caramels in the top of a double boiler over boiling water (or microwave them) until melted and smooth, stirring often. If necessary, stir in a spoonful of milk. Drop a little warm caramel on each cluster of nuts. Press a piece of bacon on top of each cluster and refrigerate 15 minutes.

Microwave the chocolate until melted and smooth, stirring every 30 seconds. Drizzle chocolate over each turtle cluster, and if you like, sprinkle with a pinch of salt while wet. Chill about 20 minutes to set chocolate. Serve at room temperature. *Makes 24 turtles.* ◑

Bacon Lover's Fudge

Ingredients

- 1 lb. bacon, diced
- 4 (4 oz.) pkgs. semi-sweet baking chocolate, chopped
- 1 (14 oz.) can sweetened condensed milk
- ¼ C. butter
- ¼ C. heavy cream
- 1 C. chopped toasted pecans

Line an 8 x 8″ baking pan with foil and coat well with cooking spray.

Cook the bacon until crisp; drain and let cool. Crumble the bacon into smaller pieces, if desired.

In a medium saucepan, combine chocolate, sweetened condensed milk, butter, and cream. Cook over medium-low heat, stirring until melted and smooth. Remove from heat. Set aside ¼ cup bacon; stir remaining bacon and all the pecans into chocolate mixture. Spread in prepared pan and sprinkle promptly with reserved bacon; press down gently. Cover and chill for 3 hours or until firm. *Makes 36 pieces.* ◖

Swinetastic Chocolate Cuppies

Ingredients

a match made in hog heaven

12 bacon strips, diced

2 C. flour

¾ C. unsweetened cocoa powder

2 C. sugar

2 tsp. baking soda

1 tsp. baking powder

½ tsp. salt

2 eggs

1 C. cold brewed coffee

1 C. buttermilk

¼ C. vegetable oil

Chocolate or vanilla frosting

2/3 full will do

Directions

Heat oven to 375°. Line 30 muffin cups with paper liners.

Cook the bacon until crisp; drain and let cool. Reserve ¼ cup bacon grease and discard the rest.

In a large bowl, whisk together the flour, cocoa powder, sugar, baking soda, baking powder, and salt. Make a well in the center and add the eggs, coffee, buttermilk, reserved bacon grease, and oil. Stir until just blended. Stir in ¾ cup bacon pieces and reserve remaining bacon for garnishing cupcakes. Spoon batter into liners, filling about ⅔ full. Bake 20 to 25 minutes or until tops spring back when lightly pressed. Cool in the pan. Spread frosting on cupcakes and sprinkle with reserved bacon. *Makes 30 cupcakes.* ❂

fun fact
You can celebrate International Bacon Day each year on the Saturday before Labor Day – Go Hog-Wild!

Squawk & Squeal Wrap-Ups

Ingredients

1¼ lbs. boneless skinless
   chicken breasts

1 lb. bacon strips

⅔ C. brown sugar

2 T. chili powder

These should
spice things up!

Directions

Heat oven to 350°. Line a rimmed baking sheet with foil and place a wire rack on top. Coat rack with cooking spray. Soak wooden skewers in water for 30 minutes.

Cut chicken into 1″ cubes. Cut bacon strips into thirds, wrap each piece around a chicken cube, and slide several onto each skewer.

Mix brown sugar and chili powder in a shallow bowl. Coat wrapped chicken pieces in brown sugar mixture and arrange skewers on prepared rack. Bake 30 to 35 minutes or until bacon is crisp. *Makes about 45 appetizers.*

Surf & Turf Bundles

Ingredients

1 lb. extra-large frozen deveined cooked shrimp, thawed, tails removed (26 to 30 shrimp)

26 to 30 fresh pineapple chunks (¼" to ½" thick)

13 to 15 thin bacon strips, cut in half

Prepared sweet & sour sauce and/or BBQ sauce

Coarse black pepper

Crushed red pepper flakes

Finely chopped chives

Soak 26 to 30 wooden skewers in water for 30 minutes. Heat oven to 425°. Line a rimmed baking sheet with foil and coat heavily with cooking spray.

Stack together one shrimp and one pineapple chunk and wrap the stack securely with a piece of bacon; push a skewer through the whole thing to secure. Arrange on prepared pan and brush sauce over each bundle. Bake for 12 minutes.

Remove from oven and brush with additional sauce; sprinkle with pepper, pepper flakes, and chives. Move skewers slightly so they don't stick to the foil. Bake 12 minutes more or until bacon is done. *Makes about 30 appetizers.*

Smokin' Hot Tots

Heat oven to 425°. Line a pan with foil and set a greased rack on top. Cut off stem end from 3 large jalapeño peppers and remove seeds. Slice peppers into ½" rings. Cut **8 thin bacon strips** into thirds. Slip a tater tot through each pepper ring (or just stack them together). Wrap with a bacon piece and secure with a toothpick. Bake on the rack for 25 to 30 minutes, until bacon is crisp. Stir crumbled cooked bacon into your favorite cheese sauce and serve alongside. *Makes 24 appetizers.* ◖

Bacon Water Chestnuts

Heat oven to 375°. Cut **1 lb. thin bacon strips** into thirds. Drain 2 (8 oz.) cans whole water chestnuts. Wrap a bacon piece around each chestnut and secure with a toothpick. Bake them in a shallow dish 25 to 30 minutes. Remove chestnuts and drain on paper towels; wipe out dish. Mix ¾ C. brown sugar, 1 T. mayonnaise, ¾ C. ketchup, and 1 tsp. Worcestershire sauce in the same dish. Set chestnuts in sauce, turn to coat, and bake 25 to 30 minutes more, until bacon is crisp. *Makes 45 appetizers.* ◖

Snout & Kraut Dijon Nachos

Ingredients

1 (14.5 oz.) can plus
  1 (8 oz.) can sauerkraut

1 C. mayonnaise

3 T. Dijon mustard

¾ tsp. coarse black pepper

½ tsp. garlic powder

½ tsp. onion powder

8 thick cut bacon strips, chopped

1 onion, chopped

1 (14 oz.) pkg. kielbasa, diced

½ each red and green bell pepper, diced

1 (13 oz.) bag tortilla chips

4 C. finely shredded mozzarella cheese

Crisp tortilla chips?
How could you refuse?

Directions

Heat oven to 350°. Drain sauerkraut, reserving 2 teaspoons juice. Place sauerkraut on a clean kitchen towel; roll up and squeeze out excess juice. Set aside.

In a medium bowl, mix the mayonnaise, mustard, pepper, garlic powder, onion powder, and reserved sauerkraut juice; cover and chill.

Cook bacon in a large skillet until crisp. Remove the bacon, drain well, and let cool. Reserve 2 tablespoons bacon grease in the skillet and add onion; sauté over medium heat for 5 minutes, stirring occasionally. Add kielbasa and cook 3 minutes more. Stir in bacon, set-aside sauerkraut, and bell peppers; cook 3 minutes more and remove from heat.

Line a large rimmed baking sheet (at least 12" x 18" x 1") with foil and coat with cooking spray. Dump tortilla chips in an even layer on the pan and sprinkle with cheese. Spoon the sauerkraut mixture evenly over the cheese. Bake 15 to 20 minutes or until the cheese melts and sauerkraut begins to turn light golden brown. Serve with the chilled mayonnaise mixture. *Makes enough for a litter of your closest friends.* ()

Ingredients

4 bacon strips

1 sheet frozen puff pastry, thawed (from a 17.3 oz. pkg.)

1 egg, beaten

1½ C. fresh baby spinach

Salt, black pepper, and ground nutmeg

¼ C. feta or shredded Gruyère cheese

1 T. grated Parmesan cheese

Heat oven to 425°. Cook the bacon until crisp; drain and let cool. Crumble the bacon and discard the grease.

Unfold the pastry and roll out according to package directions. Set dough on an ungreased cookie sheet and fold over all edges to make a rim. Brush pastry with egg and bake 10 to 12 minutes or until lightly browned (pastry will puff up). Remove from oven and press down lightly with the back of a spoon.

Arrange spinach over partially baked pastry and sprinkle with bacon. Season with salt, pepper, and nutmeg. Top with feta and Parmesan cheeses. Bake about 15 minutes, until crust is golden brown, cheese melts, and spinach wilts. Cut into squares and serve hot or at room temperature. *Makes 8 appetizers.* ◖

Puffy Pig Crumbles

Ingredients

1 lb. bacon, diced

1 (17.3 oz.) pkg. frozen
puff pastry sheets,
thawed (2 ct.)

1 C. finely shredded
Cheddar cheese

Ranch dip

Chopped fresh chives

Heat oven to 400°. Cook the bacon until crisp; drain and
let cool. Discard the grease.

On a lightly floured surface, unfold one pastry sheet and roll it
into a 12˝ square. Cut into 36 (2˝) squares and arrange them
on a cookie sheet. Poke holes in each pastry square with a fork.
Repeat with the remaining pastry sheet. Bake 8 to 10 minutes or
until pastries are golden brown. Let cool 10 minutes. With the
back of a melon baller, press down on the center of each pastry
to make a hole for the filling.

Spoon about ½ teaspoon each cheese and bacon onto each
pastry. Bake 5 minutes or until cheese melts. Transfer pastries
to a cooling rack to cool for 10 minutes. Top with a little dip and
some chives before serving. *Makes 72 appetizers.* ◗

Porker Pineapple Quesadillas

Ingredients

½ lb. bacon strips, chopped

4 (10") flour tortillas,
  any variety

1 C. finely shredded
  mozzarella cheese

½ C. diced fresh pineapple

Thinly sliced red onion

Barbecue sauce

Try not to cry... there's BACON in your future.

Directions

Cook the bacon until crisp; drain and let cool. Discard the grease.

Set a 10" skillet over medium heat and when hot, coat with cooking spray. Set one tortilla in the skillet and cover half of it with ¼ each of the cheese, pineapple, bacon, and onion. Drizzle lightly with about 1 tablespoon barbecue sauce. When cheese is melted and tortilla is golden brown, fold tortilla in half, flatten lightly, and cook about 1 minute more. Remove quesadilla to a cutting board and let cool slightly before cutting into three wedges. Repeat with remaining ingredients. Serve with barbecue sauce. *Makes 12 appetizers.*

Feeds 12

23

Ingredients

7 bacon strips, diced

Vegetable oil

½ C. popping corn

3 T. sugar

Salt

Cook the bacon until crisp; drain and let cool. Reserve the grease.

Measure the reserved bacon grease and add enough vegetable oil to equal ¼ cup. Pour grease mixture into a heavy 5-quart pot with a lid and set over medium-high heat. Add popping corn and sprinkle with sugar. Stir quickly before covering pot with the lid. Shake the pot back and forth as corn begins to pop. Remove from heat when popping slows down. Season with salt and add the bacon; toss well and serve hot. *Makes 16 cups.*

fun fact
Center-cut sliced bacon is naturally leaner than other cuts, like slab bacon.

Soused Sow Party Mix

Ingredients

8 bacon strips, coarsely chopped

1 (15 oz.) pkg. traditional Chex cereal snack mix

1 C. pecan halves

½ C. butter

½ C. brown sugar

¼ C. light corn syrup

2 T. bourbon

¾ tsp. chipotle chili powder

Heat oven to 300°. Line two rimmed baking sheets with foil. Coat foil with cooking spray and set aside.

Cook bacon until crisp; drain and let cool. Discard the grease. In a large bowl, toss together snack mix, pecans, and bacon; set aside.

In a large saucepan, combine butter, brown sugar, and corn syrup. Cook over medium heat, stirring occasionally, until bubbles form around edges. Cook 5 minutes more and then remove from heat. Let cool for 2 minutes. Carefully stir in bourbon and chili powder; pour over the snack mixture and toss until evenly coated. Spread on prepared pans and bake 15 minutes, stirring every 5 minutes. Cool completely. *Makes 10 cups.* ◑

Hogs & Kisses Cookies

Ingredients

Bacon!
Delicious even
in cookies!

5 bacon strips

2½ C. flour

½ tsp. baking soda

½ tsp. salt

½ C. butter, softened

½ C. shortening

½ C. sugar

1 C. brown sugar

2 eggs

1 tsp. vanilla

1 tsp. maple extract

1 C. mini chocolate chips

Chocolate Kisses (about 48)

Directions

Heat oven to 350°. Line cookie sheets with parchment paper.

Cook bacon until crisp; drain and let cool. Crumble the bacon and discard the grease.

Whisk together the flour, baking soda, and salt; set aside. In a large mixing bowl, beat together the butter, shortening, sugar, and brown sugar on medium speed until smooth. Beat in eggs. Add vanilla and maple extract; beat until blended. Gradually stir in the flour mixture with a spoon until just combined. Fold in the bacon and chocolate chips.

Drop by spoonful onto prepared cookie sheets and bake 10 to 12 minutes or until lightly browned around edges. Remove from oven and press a chocolate Kiss in the center of each cookie; return to the oven to bake 1 minute more. Let cool several minutes on cookie sheets before transferring to a rack to cool completely. *Makes about 4 dozen cookies.*

an incredible mix of salty and sweet to satisfy your cravings

Bloomin' Bacon Ranch Bread

Ingredients

8 bacon strips

1 round loaf sourdough bread, unsliced

2½ to 3 C. shredded sharp Cheddar cheese

6 T. butter, melted

1 heaping T. dry ranch dressing mix

2 T. chopped green onion

Ranch dressing for dipping

Cut it deep, it'll forgive you.

Directions

Heat oven to 350°. Line a cookie sheet with foil (large enough to cover bread). Cook bacon until crisp; drain and let cool. Crumble the bacon and discard the grease.

Slice the bread lengthwise and widthwise without cutting through the bottom crust (make cuts about 1˝ apart). Set bread on the foil. Sprinkle cheese and bacon between the cuts in bread. Stir together the butter, dressing mix, and green onion; drizzle between cuts and over bread. Wrap the foil around bread and seal all edges. Bake 15 minutes. Open foil and bake bread 5 to 10 minutes more or until cheese melts. Serve immediately with a side of ranch dressing.
Makes 8 servings. ◗

Fill-the-Trough Spiced Nuts

Ingredients

1¼ C. brown sugar

12 bacon strips

2 T. vegetable oil

3½ C. sugar

4 C. raw nuts (any variety)

1 T. plus 1 tsp. salt

2 tsp. garam masala

1 tsp. ground cumin

⅛ tsp. ground cinnamon

⅛ tsp. ground allspice

1½ tsp. cayenne pepper

Heat oven to 350°. Line a rimmed baking sheet with foil. Sprinkle half the brown sugar over the foil; lay bacon on top and sprinkle with remaining brown sugar. Oven-roast the bacon for 25 to 40 minutes or until caramelized, flipping strips several times. Transfer bacon to a clean tray to cool completely.

Increase oven temperature to 400°. Line a clean rimmed baking sheet with foil and brush with oil; set aside.

Combine sugar and 3 cups water in a saucepan and bring to a boil over high heat. Reduce heat and stir in nuts and all seasonings; simmer for 8 minutes. Remove nuts and drain well. Spread nuts on the oiled pan and roast them in the oven for 12 to 15 minutes or until golden brown, stirring once. Cool completely. Chop the caramelized bacon and toss with the roasted nuts. *Makes 5 cups.* ❤

Piggy Ranch Popcorn

Ingredients

6 bacon strips, diced

Vegetable oil

¾ C. popping corn

1 (.4 oz.) pkg. dry ranch
  dressing mix

Cook the bacon until crisp; drain and let cool. Reserve
the grease.

Measure the reserved bacon grease and add enough vegetable
oil to equal ½ cup. Pour grease mixture into a heavy 6-quart pot
with a lid. Set the pot over medium-high heat and add popping
corn; cover with the lid and shake the pot back and forth as corn
begins to pop. Remove from heat when popping slows down.
Transfer popped corn into a large bowl. Sprinkle with dressing
mix and add bacon; toss well. *Makes 24 cups.*

fun fact

Can't get enough bacon? You can buy
bacon-flavored toothpaste, gumballs, or
lip balm to satisfy the cravings.

Feeds 8

Little Piggy Quiche Cups

Ingredients

1 refrigerated pie crust, softened (from a 14.1 oz. pkg.)

3 oz. cream cheese, softened

1 egg plus 1 egg yolk

¼ C. chopped green onion

⅔ C. shredded Swiss cheese

8 precooked bacon strips, chopped

Use a handy dandy cutter for quick circles.

Directions

Heat oven to 425°. Grease 16 mini muffin cups with cooking spray and set aside.

Unroll pie crust on a lightly floured surface. Use a 2½˝ cookie cutter to cut about 16 rounds from the crust, rerolling scraps as needed. Press one round into each prepared muffin cup, patting down gently to form a pastry cup.

In a blender container or food processor bowl, combine cream cheese, egg, egg yolk, and green onion. Process until almost smooth. Divide mixture evenly among crust cups (about 2 teaspoons each). Top with some Swiss cheese and bacon. Bake about 15 minutes or until edges are lightly browned. Cool for 5 minutes before removing cups from pan. *Makes 16 appetizers.*

You can buy fully cooked bacon strips that are ready to use – or precook them yourself.

Pig-Out Gooey Brownies

Ingredients

½ lb. bacon, diced

Melted butter

2 (1 oz.) squares
   unsweetened chocolate,
   chopped

1¼ C. sugar

2 eggs, lightly beaten

2 tsp. vanilla

¼ tsp. salt

½ C. flour

1 C. heavy cream

2 C. dark chocolate chips

Directions

Heat oven to 325°. Coat an 8 x 8″ baking pan with cooking spray. Cook the bacon until crisp; drain and let cool. Reserve the grease. Add enough butter to the reserved grease to equal ½ cup. Combine grease mixture and chopped chocolate in a saucepan and stir over medium heat until melted. Remove from heat and stir in sugar; let cool slightly. Whisk in eggs, vanilla, and salt. Fold in flour until smooth.

Pour half the batter into prepared pan and sprinkle with half the bacon. Spread remaining batter on top. Bake 20 minutes; sprinkle with some of remaining bacon (reserve some for the topping). Bake 10 to 15 minutes more or until brownies test done with a toothpick. Let cool completely.

Heat cream in a saucepan to nearly scalding, but do not boil. Remove from heat and add chocolate chips; let rest until melted. Whisk smooth and cool slightly before pouring over brownies. Top with remaining bacon. *Makes 16 brownies.* ◖

Bacon-Wrapped Brat Bites

Ingredients

4 bratwurst

3 (12 oz.) cans light beer

5 T. brown sugar

1 tsp. cayenne pepper

8 to 10 bacon strips, cut in half

Poke each bratwurst several times and place them in a saucepan with the beer. Bring to a boil over high heat. Reduce heat to medium and simmer 15 minutes. Remove brats and let rest until cool enough to handle.

Heat oven to 425°. Line a rimmed baking sheet with foil and set a rack on top. Mix brown sugar and cayenne pepper in a large bowl. Cut each bratwurst into 1½″ pieces and wrap a piece of bacon around each brat section; secure with toothpicks. Toss the wrapped brats with the cayenne mixture until coated and place on the rack. Bake until bacon is brown and crisp, 23 to 30 minutes. Serve warm with your favorite sauce or dip. *Makes 16 appetizers.*

Piggly-Wiggly Sticks

Heat oven to 375° and line a cookie sheet with foil. Mix ½ C. grated Parmesan cheese, 1 tsp. garlic powder, and ½ tsp. coarse black pepper. Dredge one side of **12 thin bacon strips** in the cheese mixture. Separate the breadsticks from 1 (11 oz.) refrigerated tube and stretch each one to 9" long. Wrap a bacon strip around each, cheese side against dough. Place on cookie sheet and press down on the ends of breadsticks. Bake 15 to 20 minutes or until golden brown. Sprinkle with remaining cheese mixture and let cool. *Makes 12 sticks.* ◖

Oinky-Doink Dates

Heat oven to 425° and line a rimmed pan with foil. Pipe ¼ C. softened cream cheese spread into the hole of 24 pitted dates. Cut **8 thin maple bacon strips** into thirds. Wrap each bacon piece around a filled date and secure with a toothpick. Dredge in ¼ C. brown sugar. Set on prepared pan and drizzle with maple syrup. Bake about 10 minutes; turn dates and bake 8 to 10 minutes more or until bacon is brown and crisp. Serve warm. *Makes 24 appetizers.* ◖

Feeds 6

Roly-Poly Egg Rolls

Ingredients

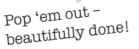

12 bacon strips, cut in half

2 large fresh avocados

½ fresh lime, juiced

Salt

1 T. flour

12 egg roll wrappers

Sliced Pepper Jack cheese

Canola oil for frying

Pop 'em out –
beautifully done!

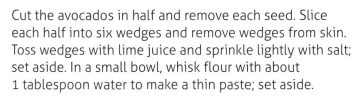

Tuck them in, nice and cozy!

Directions

Cook the bacon strips until almost crisp; drain and let cool. Discard the grease.

Cut the avocados in half and remove each seed. Slice each half into six wedges and remove wedges from skin. Toss wedges with lime juice and sprinkle lightly with salt; set aside. In a small bowl, whisk flour with about 1 tablespoon water to make a thin paste; set aside.

Place one egg roll wrapper on a plate with a corner pointing toward you (forming a diamond shape). Place a piece of cheese in the middle, topped with an avocado slice, two bacon pieces, another avocado slice and another piece of cheese. Fold the point of the egg roll wrapper nearest you over the food in the center. Fold the left and right points over the middle and then roll up the wrapper nearly all the way, folding tightly to enclose ingredients. Moisten the remaining corner of wrapper with the flour paste and press to seal egg roll. Repeat to make 11 more egg rolls.

In a heavy saucepan, heat 2˝ of oil to 350°. In small batches, fry egg rolls in hot oil until golden brown, about 5 minutes, turning once partway through cooking time. Drain well on paper towels and serve with your favorite dip or sauce.
Makes 12 appetizers. ◖

Alfredo's Wild Hog Pizza

Ingredients

1 (13.8 oz.) tube refrigerated
pizza dough

1 C. bacon flavored or plain
Alfredo sauce

1¼ C. shredded mozzarella
cheese, divided

1 (10 oz.) pkg. frozen chopped
spinach, thawed and squeezed dry

2 or 3 plum tomatoes, thinly sliced

5 precooked bacon strips

Look... you
can eat your
veggies too.

Directions

Heat oven to 425°. Coat a 12˝ to 14˝ pizza pan with cooking
spray and set aside.

Unroll dough and press evenly into prepared pan, making
a small rim around outer edge. Spread sauce over dough.
Sprinkle with ½ cup cheese. Top with the spinach and
tomatoes. Cut bacon into 1˝ pieces and arrange them over
the pizza. Sprinkle remaining ¾ cup cheese on top. Bake
about 15 minutes or until crust is golden brown and cheese
is melted. Cut into small squares. *Makes enough for lots of
little piggies.*

Bacon & Blue Pig Skins

Ingredients

6 bacon strips

½ lb. lean ground beef

4 whole Russet potatoes,
  baked until done

3 T. butter, melted

Salt and black pepper

½ C. crumbled blue cheese,
  divided

Line a broiler pan with foil and set aside. Cook bacon until crisp; drain and let cool. Crumble the bacon and discard the grease. Meanwhile, brown the ground beef until crumbly and set aside.

Cool the baked potatoes about 15 minutes. Cut potatoes in half lengthwise. Scoop out some of the insides, leaving a sturdy shell. (Reserve the insides for another use.)

Preheat broiler to high heat. Brush butter over both sides of each shell and set on prepared pan; season with salt and pepper. Place under broiler for 6 to 10 minutes or until slightly crisp. Remove from oven and spoon some of the cooked beef, bacon, and about 1 tablespoon cheese into each shell. Broil 2 to 3 minutes more or until cheese is bubbly. Top with more cheese and cut in half before serving, if desired. *Makes 8 to 16 appetizers.* ◖

Boss Hog's Sweet Tater Skins

Ingredients

3 bacon strips

3 large sweet potatoes

2 T. olive oil

¼ each red and green bell pepper, diced

Onion powder

Garlic salt

Black pepper

Parmesan cheese

Honey, optional

Preheat oven to 400°. Line a large rimmed baking sheet with foil and set aside.

Cook bacon until crisp; drain and let cool. Crumble the bacon and discard the grease.

Poke holes in the sweet potatoes and cook in the microwave for 7 to 9 minutes or until tender. Let cool 5 minutes; slice potatoes lengthwise into four equal "boats." Scoop out some of the insides, leaving a shell. (Reserve the insides for another use.)

Place potato shells on prepared pan and brush oil over both sides of each shell. Top each one with some bacon and bell peppers. Season with onion powder, garlic salt, pepper, and Parmesan cheese. Bake 24 minutes. Drizzle with honey before serving, if desired. *Makes 12 appetizers.* ◑

Crabby Little Bacon Cups

Ingredients

Say, "Cheese please!"

1 lb. thin bacon strips

1 (8 oz.) pkg. cream cheese, softened

4 (6 oz.) cans crabmeat, drained well

1 C. shredded Cheddar cheese

2 tsp. Old Bay Seasoning

1 tsp. dry mustard

½ tsp. onion powder

Salt and black pepper

Paprika

A love fest: bacon-hugged crabmeat and cheese!

Directions

Heat oven to 400°. Cut bacon strips into fourths. Arrange two pieces of bacon inside a mini muffin cup to create a liner to hold the filling. Repeat to line 36 cups and set aside.

Stir together cream cheese, crabmeat, Cheddar cheese, Old Bay Seasoning, dry mustard, and onion powder. Season with salt and pepper and stir until well blended. Fill each bacon cup with a rounded teaspoonful of crab mixture and press down to completely fill cups. Sprinkle lightly with paprika. Bake 20 to 25 minutes or until lightly browned and bacon reaches desired crispness. Let cool in pan for 5 to 7 minutes. Carefully remove bacon cups from the pan and drain well on paper towels. Serve warm with sour cream, if you like. *Makes 36 appetizers.* ◖

flavor fact
Some favorite bacon flavors include peppered, applewood, maple, mesquite, honey-maple, and hickory smoked.

Pork Poppers in a Blanket

Ingredients

4 (3″) jalapeño peppers, stemmed

⅓ C. chive and onion cream cheese spread

6 precooked bacon strips, cut into thirds

1 (8 oz.) tube refrigerated crescent rolls

½ C. pineapple or fruit salsa

Just the "kick" these hogs need!

Directions

Heat oven to 375°. Slice each jalapeño in half lengthwise; remove and discard seeds. Then cut in half crosswise. Spoon about 1 teaspoon cheese spread into each jalapeño section and set a piece of bacon on top.

Unroll crescent roll dough and separate into eight triangles. Cut each triangle in half lengthwise, making 16 long narrow triangles. Set a filled jalapeño, bacon side down, on the widest end of a dough triangle. Roll up dough around jalapeño and set on an ungreased cookie sheet. Repeat to make 16. Bake 12 to 15 minutes or until golden brown. Serve promptly with salsa. *Makes 16 appetizers.*

Sizzling Bacon Bread Bowl

Ingredients

7 bacon strips

1 round loaf bread, unsliced

2 C. shredded Monterey Jack cheese

1 C. shredded Parmesan cheese

1 C. mayonnaise

¼ C. finely diced onion

½ tsp. minced garlic

¼ tsp. crushed red pepper flakes

Heat oven to 350°. Cook bacon until crisp; drain and let cool. Crumble the bacon and discard the grease.

Slice the top ¼ off the bread loaf and set it aside. Hollow out the inside of loaf to make a bread bowl with a 1″ shell. Cube the removed bread and reserve it to serve with the dip.

Stir together both cheeses, mayonnaise, onion, bacon, garlic, and pepper flakes. Spoon mixture into the bread bowl. Cover dip with loaf top and bake on an ungreased cookie sheet for 45 minutes or until heated through. Serve with the reserved bread cubes, crackers, or corn chips. *Feeds a litter of your best friends.*

Ingredients

- ½ lb. ground beef
- **8 bacon strips, diced**
- ½ C. diced onion
- ½ tsp. minced garlic
- 4 oz. cream cheese, softened
- ½ C. sour cream
- ¼ C. mayonnaise
- ½ C. shredded mozzarella cheese
- ½ C. shredded Cheddar cheese
- 1 T. Worcestershire sauce
- 2 T. ketchup

Heat oven to 350°. In a skillet, cook ground beef over medium heat until crumbly; drain. Cook bacon in the same skillet until crisp. Remove the bacon and drain well. Reserve 1½ tablespoons bacon grease in the skillet and discard the rest. Sauté onion and garlic in the bacon grease until tender and then set aside.

In a large bowl, mix the cream cheese, sour cream, mayonnaise, mozzarella and Cheddar cheeses, Worcestershire sauce, and ketchup. Stir in the cooked beef, bacon, and onion mixture. Transfer to a baking dish and bake 15 to 20 minutes. Serve warm with tortilla or pita chips. *Makes 2 cups dip.*

Potbellied 'Shrooms

Ingredients

1 lb. white button mushrooms

½ lb. bacon, diced

½ C. minced sweet onion

1 tsp. minced garlic

4 oz. cream cheese

¼ C. grated Parmesan cheese

Salt and black pepper

Olive oil

Don't be a pig! Save some for the 'shrooms.

Cheese & Bacon... it was meant to be!

Directions

Heat oven to 350°. Line a rimmed baking sheet with foil and set aside.

Remove mushroom stems from caps; chop stems into small pieces and set caps on prepared pan.

Cook the bacon in a skillet over medium heat until crisp. Remove bacon and drain well; crumble it into smaller pieces and set aside. Reserve 2 tablespoons bacon grease in the skillet and discard the rest. Add onion to the skillet and sauté until tender, about 5 minutes. Add chopped mushroom stems and garlic; cook and stir a few minutes more.

Reduce heat to low. Add cream cheese and Parmesan cheese to skillet, stirring until cheeses melt. Add bacon and season with salt and pepper. Remove from heat and stuff each mushroom cap generously with bacon mixture; drizzle with a little oil. Bake for 20 minutes or until mushrooms are soft and filling is hot. *Makes 24 appetizers.*

Want to chop or dice raw bacon easily? Do it with your kitchen shears!

Cheeseball Runts

Ingredients

4 to 5 bacon strips

4 oz. cream cheese, softened

1 (4 oz.) pkg. chèvre (goat) cheese

2 tsp. dried basil, divided

⅓ C. chopped pecans

Line a cookie sheet with waxed paper. Cook the bacon until crisp; drain and let cool. Crumble the bacon to measure ⅓ cup and discard the grease.

In a food processor bowl, combine both cheeses and 1 teaspoon basil; process until well mixed. Chill for 15 minutes. Shape cheese mixture into 16 small balls and set on prepared cookie sheet. If you like, insert a lollipop stick into each ball. Freeze the cheeseballs for 20 minutes.

With the clean food processor, pulse the pecans, bacon, and remaining 1 teaspoon basil until finely ground. Roll cheeseballs in the bacon mixture, pressing in place as needed. Serve immediately or chill first. *Makes 16 appetizers.*

DILL-icious Porker Packs

Ingredients

12 dill pickle spears

18 bacon strips, cut in half

Canola oil for frying

1½ C. flour

1½ T. seasoned salt

1 (12 oz.) can beer

Ranch dressing

Cut each pickle spear into three equal chunks, about 1½″ long. Wrap each chunk in one piece of bacon. Set nine wrapped pickles on a microwave-safe plate, seam side down. Microwave for 1½ to 2½ minutes, just until the bacon begins to shrink around the pickle and will not come unwrapped. Repeat until all are partially cooked; set aside.

In a heavy saucepan, heat 2″ of oil to 350°. Meanwhile, in a medium bowl, mix the flour and salt. Whisk in beer until the batter is smooth and slightly thicker than pancake batter. (Use any extra batter to coat other foods you'd like to fry.)

Dip the partially cooked pickles into the batter until well coated. Work in small batches to fry the pickles in hot oil until golden brown, about 5 minutes. Drain on paper towels and serve warm with ranch dressing. *Makes 36 appetizers.* ◗

Babe's Bruschetta

Ingredients

10 applewood smoked bacon strips

Mayonnaise

8 (¾" thick) slices French bread

Garlic powder

8 slices Swiss cheese, cut in half

2 Roma tomatoes,
   seeded and chopped

Swiss...
Mmmm
Gooood

Directions

Cook the bacon strips until crisp; drain and let cool. Crumble eight of the strips and set the remaining two strips aside. Discard the bacon grease.

Preheat broiler to high heat. Spread mayonnaise on each bread slice and set on a broiler pan, mayo side up. Broil 4" from the heat for 1 to 2 minutes or until toasted; remove from oven and sprinkle with garlic powder.

Lay a piece of cheese on each bread slice. Divide the crumbled bacon and tomatoes among the bread slices and top each with another piece of cheese. Broil 1 minute or until cheese is melted. Cut the set-aside bacon strips into eight pieces and set one on each bread slice. *Makes 8 appetizers.*

Feeds 8

Squeal Deal Apricot Squares

chop, chop...
nice and fine

Ingredients

1½ lbs. honey-maple bacon strips, coarsely chopped

20 (9 x 14˝) sheets phyllo dough (from a 16 oz. pkg.)

½ C. butter, melted

1½ C. sliced toasted almonds

¾ C. chopped dried apricots

⅓ C. apricot preserves

¾ C. honey

Directions

Heat oven to 350°. Generously coat a 9 x 13″ baking dish with cooking spray.

Cook the bacon until crisp; drain and let cool. Discard the grease.

Trim phyllo dough sheets to fit into prepared dish and cover with a damp cloth. One at a time, layer 10 phyllo sheets in the baking dish, brushing each sheet with butter before the next layer. Keep the remaining 10 dough sheets covered until needed.

With a food processor, pulse the bacon, almonds, and apricots until finely chopped. Sprinkle bacon mixture over the dough in baking dish. Top with remaining phyllo dough sheets, brushing with butter between layers as before. Butter the top sheet. Cut into diamonds or squares with a sharp knife. Bake for 30 minutes.

Meanwhile, in a saucepan, stir together the preserves and honey; simmer 1 minute. Remove baking dish from oven and pour honey mixture over all. Let cool at least 1 hour before removing from pan. Serve warm or cold. *Makes 20 appetizers.*

Aromatherapy Rx: Cook some BACON! Ahhhh...

Show-Me-The-Bacon Toffee

Ingredients

½ lb. bacon strips, diced

1 C. butter

1 C. plus 2½ T. sugar

2 T. light corn syrup

½ tsp. vanilla

Line a 9 x 13″ pan with parchment paper.

Cook the bacon until crisp; drain and let cool. Discard the grease.

In a large heavy saucepan over medium-high heat, combine the butter, sugar, corn syrup, 2 tablespoons water, and vanilla. Bring to a boil, stirring frequently. Cook until a candy thermometer reaches 300° (it goes quickly after 200°). Remove from heat and stir in the bacon. Pour immediately into prepared pan and gently spread toffee in an even layer with a spatula. Let cool completely until firm, about 30 minutes. Break into pieces. *Provides sweet bacon bliss for a bunch.* 🐾

Porky Frito Bars

Ingredients

8 to 10 bacon strips, diced

1 (10.25 oz.) bag Fritos corn chips

1 C. sugar

1 C. light corn syrup

1 C. creamy peanut butter

Crushed red pepper flakes, optional

½ C. semi-sweet chocolate chips or 2 squares chocolate almond bark

Grease a 10 x 15˝ rimmed baking sheet with cooking spray.

Cook the bacon until crisp; drain and let cool. Discard the grease. Spread the corn chips on prepared pan and sprinkle with most of the bacon (reserve some to sprinkle over the top).

In a medium saucepan, mix sugar and corn syrup; bring to a boil over medium heat while stirring. Boil for 1 minute. Remove from heat and stir in the peanut butter until smooth. Pour mixture evenly over corn chips. Sprinkle sparingly with pepper flakes, if desired.

Microwave the chocolate until melted and smooth, stirring several times. Drizzle over bars and sprinkle remaining bacon over the top. Let set up and then cut into pieces. *Feeds a hungry herd.* ❍

Sandwich Boar'd Bites

Ingredients

8 bacon strips

1 (8 oz.) tube refrigerated crescent roll dough

½ lb. deli-sliced smoked turkey

6 large slices Pepper Jack cheese

3 to 4 Roma tomatoes, thinly sliced

3 eggs, beaten

My heart belongs to bacon... but tomato is good, too.

Directions

Heat oven to 350°. Grease an 8 x 8˝ baking dish with cooking spray and set aside. Cook bacon until crisp; drain and let cool. Coarsely crumble the bacon and discard grease.

Unroll dough and separate into two squares. Press one square into prepared dish for bottom crust, sealing perforations. Layer half each of the turkey, bacon, cheese, and tomatoes over crust. Drizzle half the eggs over the top. Repeat the layers with remaining turkey, bacon, cheese, and tomatoes. Flatten remaining dough into an 8 x 8˝ square. Place dough over layers in dish and pour remaining eggs on top.

Cover with foil and bake 20 minutes. Uncover and bake 20 to 25 minutes more. Let rest at room temperature for 15 minutes before cutting into small squares. *Makes 16 mini sandwiches.* ❂

Swine & Dine Sliders

Ingredients

1 lb. hickory smoked bacon strips, chopped

¾ lb. ground beef

½ lb. ground pork

1 tsp. salt, or more to taste

2 tsp. paprika

1 tsp. dried oregano

½ tsp. black pepper

½ tsp. crushed red pepper flakes

1 egg

¼ C. barbecue sauce

¼ C. grape jelly

9 slider buns

Behold the bacon!

And a topping of chives will do nicely!

Directions

Heat oven to 400°. Coat a 9 x 9″ baking pan with cooking spray and set aside.

Cook the bacon until crisp; drain and let cool. With a food processor, pulse the bacon until finely chopped. Transfer bacon to a large bowl and add beef, pork, salt, paprika, oregano, pepper, pepper flakes, and egg. Mix until well combined.

Gently press mixture into prepared pan. Bake about 25 minutes or until meat is cooked through.

Meanwhile, combine barbecue sauce and grape jelly in a saucepan over low heat, stirring until glaze is warm and blended. Baste meat with the glaze during the last 5 minutes of cooking time. Cut into nine pieces and serve on buns with the extra glaze on the side. *Makes 9 sliders.*

When a recipe tells you to cook 8 or more bacon strips, either bake the whole strips in a large pan or cut them up before frying in a skillet, so you can cook all the bacon at once. Swinefully simple!

Index